Gabriel

Gabriel

A POEM

Edward Hirsch

ALFRED A. KNOPF · *New York* · 2016

THIS IS A BORZOI BOOK
PUBLISHED BY ALFRED A. KNOPF

Copyright © 2014 by Edward Hirsch

Grateful acknowledgment is made to Sony/ATV Music
Publishing LLC for permission to reprint an excerpt from
"Strings," written by Tom DeLonge, Mark Hoppus, and
Scott Raynor, copyright © 1993 EMI April Music Inc.,
Jolly Old Saint Dick and Publisher(s) Unknown. All rights
on behalf of EMI April Music Inc. and Jolly Old Saint Dick
administered by Sony/ATV Music Publishing LLC, 424 Church
Street, Suite 1200, Nashville, TN 37219. All rights reserved.
Reprinted by permission.

Library of Congress Cataloging-in-Publication Data
Hirsch, Edward.
Gabriel : a poem / by Edward Hirsch.—First edition.
pages cm
ISBN 978-0-385-35373-1 (hardcover)—ISBN 978-0-8041-7287-5 (trade pbk.)—
ISBN 978-0-385-35358-8 (eBook) 1. Children—Death—Poetry.
2. Grief—Poetry. I. Title.
PS3558.I64G33 2014
811'.54—dc23   2013049301

Cover design by Oliver Munday

Published September 3, 2014
First Paperback Edition, March 1, 2016

I would do anything and that's
What scares me so bad
Don't want to live my life alone
Don't want to go back to what I had

Don't want to spend my life without
All those special things
Don't want to walk around being tied to
Anyone else's

Strings, strings, strings, strings

BLINK-182, "Strings"

Gabriel

The funeral director opened the coffin
And there he was alone
From the waist up

I peered down into his face
And for a moment I was taken aback
Because it was not Gabriel

It was just some poor kid
Whose face looked like a room
That had been vacated

But then I looked more intently
At his heavy eyelids
And fine features

He had always been a restive sleeper
Now he was weirdly still
My reckless boy

Dressed up for a special occasion
He liked that navy-blue suit
And preened over himself in the mirror

Hey college boy the guy called out
On the street in Northampton
You look sharp in those new duds

He loved the way he looked
After he stopped taking the meds
That fogged his mind

He admired himself
In store windows and revolving doors
Where his reflection turned

Now he looked rigid and buttoned up
Like he was going to a funeral
On a Friday in early September

✦

Laurie loosened his necktie
And opened his top button
So I could breathe easier

His face was waxen
And slightly shiny
His skin gray and papery

Why were there black marks
Around his eyes
Already a little sunken

His nose slightly deformed
A scab where his lip had bled
During the seizure

He was still handsome
In his fresh haircut but something
Was off he wasn't moving

He could never stand still but now
Something that had once been my son
Lay there restless spirit

Who left the house one rainy night
And never returned
Lost boy

Who will never be found again
Anywhere but eternity
Uncontrollable fiery youth

Who whirled into any room
And ranted against whatever
Came into his mind

The world was unjust to him
And so he hurled his tirades
And then disappeared

✦

He has the Japanese word for music
Tattooed on one arm and a Jewish star
Tattooed on the other

It looks colored in with blue crayon
You shall not make gashes in your flesh
For the dead or incise any marks on yourselves

I am the Lord it says in Leviticus
But something tribal had taken root
And he labeled himself a Jew

He downed all four glasses of wine
And sold me the afikomen on Passover
But he did not like the High Holidays

He disliked Sunday school
He was allergic to synagogues
I never saw him crack a prayer book

When he was too young to object
Janet dressed him up for Purim
In a black and white shirt

With a sign on his back that said
Queen Esther's Little Brother
He roared a noisemaker against Haman

I wonder what he would think
About the short-sleeved shroud
He is wearing under his white shirt

In the casket I hope it's comfortable
He would have scorned the old Jew
We hired to sit with him overnight

Janet didn't want him to be by himself
I'm sure he was annoyed by the prayers
I wonder if he believed in God I never asked

◆

He once cut the grass around Emily Dickinson's grave
In West Cemetery in downtown Amherst
And read me the inscription *Called Back*

It reminded him of going to the cemetery
In Houston to visit his friend
Who was now in heaven Lettie said

He experienced the rapture
But Gabriel talked to the gravestone
And clutched a reindeer with a yellow bandana

I wonder if he knelt down and prayed
With the family when his friend died of leukemia
Cousins rolled in the aisle speaking in tongues

Jews stand up to the Almighty
I told him but mostly we just skipped
Out of services and headed to the playground

He was named after Janet's mother Gertrude
And the angel Gabriel
Strong man of God

He had three epileptic seizures
Suddenly his brain caught fire
He spasmed to the ground and blanked out

Dostoevsky believed the convulsive fits
Bring you down bring you closer
The idiot the holy fool are nearer to God

He was a pallbearer at two funerals
One of my fathers died in Chicago
One in Phoenix I gave both eulogies

The music of death is solemn
He kept hugging me afterward and talked
Like a madman in the car to the graveyard

✦

Like a spear hurtling through darkness
He was always in such a hurry
To find a target to stop him

Like a young lion trying out its roar
At the far edge of the den
The roar inside him was even louder

Like a bolt of lightning in the fog
Like a bolt of lightning over the sea
Like a bolt of lightning in our backyard

Like the time I opened the furnace
In the factory at night
And the flames came blasting out

I was unprepared for the intensity
Of the heat escaping
As if I'd unsheathed the sun

Like a crazed fly the daredevil monarch
Like a bee exploding from its hive
Like a bird ricocheting off the window

Like a small car zooming too fast
On a two-lane highway at night
His friends thought they would die

Like the war cry of an injured crane
Falling into the sea
I did not see it hit the waves

Like the stray fury of a bullet
Splintering against a skull
The soldier looked surprised

He did not move when they touched him
Like a bolt of lightning flooded with darkness
After it strikes the sea

◆

Ben Jonson was off in the country
Visiting a friend's estate
When he had a vision

Of his eldest son Benjamin
Who appeared to him with the mark
Of a bloody cross on his forehead

As if it had been cut with a sword
Jonson was so amazed
By the apparition that he prayed

Unto God it was but a fantasy
His friends assured him
It was a fevered dream

It was no dream
The letter came from his wife
Announcing their seven-year-old son

Had died of the Pest
Ravaging London in 1603
Why had the father escaped

That night Jonson's son appeared
To him again in a dream
This time the child of his right hand

Had grown into the shape of a man
The one he would become
On the Day of Resurrection

Jonson wrote a poem and called his son
His best piece of poetrie
A lovely line a little loathsome

I loved that poem once
He said we are lent our sons never take
Too much pleasure in what you love

◆

Why go over seven years of fertility
Doctors medicine men in clinics
Peddling surgeries and drugs

Why go over seven years of treatments
That never engendered a child
Janet and I adopted him

It took another twelve months
Of social workers and lawyers
Home studies and courtrooms

Passports and interlocutory orders
Injunctions jurisdictions handshakes
Everyone standing around in suits

Saying *yes we think so yes*
What was for others nature
Was for us culture

We traveled from Rome to New Orleans
It took twenty-three hours
Of anguish and airplanes

Instructions in two languages
Music from cream-colored headsets
Jet lag instead of labor

On the other end a rainbow
Of streamers in the French Quarter
A celebration in Jackson Square

We stayed in an empty bungalow
And waited all night
By the bay-shaped window

For the moment when our lawyer
Collected him from the hospital
And brought him to us

✦

It was inscribed
In the Book of Life
And the court of law

It was signed in a neighboring parish
And written in black ink
It was sealed in blood

After five days and nights
On this earth our lawyer
Took him from the arms of a nurse

Strapped him into an infant seat
And delivered him
Into our keeping

A wrinkled traveler
From faraway who had journeyed
A great distance to find us

A sweet aboriginal angel
With his own life a throbbing bundle
Of instincts and nerves

Perfect fingers perfect toes
Shiny skin blue soulful eyes
Deeply set in a perfectly shaped head

He was a trumpet of laughter
And tears who did not sleep
Through the night even once

O little swimmer in the deeps
Raise up your arms
Ring out your lungs

O wailing messenger
O baleful full-bodied crier
Of the abandoned and the chosen

◆

He dropped out of the sky
Into the infirmary in the Garden District
At nine pounds two ounces

When he was eight days old
We carried him into family court
In a plastic molded seat with a handle

After he settled our case with a special order
The judge an amateur photographer
Snapped pictures of us in the witness stand

We propped him up in the middle
Of the table in a Chinese restaurant
And rotated him this way and that

The mohel arrived at my parents' apartment
With a little black suitcase of instruments
It was barbaric but it was our barbarism

At the American Academy in Rome
Our friends threw a black-and-white party
Like Truman Capote he wore black and white booties

There were *Welcome Gabriel* signs in the rafters
The classicists drank gallons of red wine
And hoisted him up like a trophy

Gelsa the Italian nanny overdressed him
And took him all over Trastevere he was known
At the butcher shops the dry cleaners the coffee bars

He had become the unofficial mayor
Of the neighborhood waving from his stroller
At shopkeepers who waved and shouted *Ciao Gabriele*

When he learned to crawl he pulled himself
Forward on his arms a little at a time
As if he were climbing Utah Beach on D-day

◆

We strapped him into the car seat
And drove around for hours
Trying to get him to sleep

There were other parents nodding
To each other on the road I remember steering
Clear of the trucks veering down Highway 59

Give him a wing and a propeller
And he'll launch I joked
When he hurled himself out of his crib

It was no joke when he twitched
And twisted in his sleep we marveled
That he never stopped moving

I can make out a man pushing a stroller
Through Rice Village on Sunday morning
Dew on the grass mist on the windows

The moon a crescent in a children's book
The streets vacant the parking lots empty
Everyone in the city slept but us

Why all the tears
Oh blow Gabriel blow
Go on and blow Gabriel blow

At the diner we set him up in a high chair
Where the little pasha shrieked
And littered the floor below

While Little Richard mimicked a drum intro
From the speakers above
A-wop-bop-a-loo-bop-a-lop-bop-bop

In the end it becomes a blur
Oh blow Gabriel blow
Go on and blow Gabriel blow

◆

Issa recalled how a young priest
Slipped crossing a bridge
And fell into the torrents of a river

People searched with lighted torches
Until they found him wedged between rocks
And carried him home on a litter

His parents wept they wept bitterly
In front of everyone and even the old priests
Cried until their sleeves were soaked in tears

When the boy was cremated two days later
Issa tossed flowers into the flames
And watched them seeping into the sky

He lost three baby boys in infancy
He named his daughter Sato
Hoping she would grow in wisdom

She was pure moonlight beaming
From head to foot a butterfly
Resting her wings on a sprig of grass

He believed his two-year-old flitted
In a special state of grace
With divine protection from Buddha

But he was wrong he could not bear
To see her body swollen with blisters
In the clutches of the vile god of smallpox

His wife cried at her death he did not
He tried to escape he could not
Cut the binding cord of human love

The world of dew
Is the world of dew
And yet and yet

◆

I pulled to the side of the road
When he announced that we bought him
From a special baby store

He came home from preschool
And opened the refrigerator
Where's my fucking milk

It was not his birthday
But he kept blowing out the candles
On his cousin's cake

He wheeled his tricycle up and down
In front of the house in a rage
You're not my parents

Sometimes Gabriel and our dog raced
Back and forth across the museum lawn
Until Rocky got tired out

Curators paused to watch him run
With so much energy he was like a wound top
He could almost fly a kite when there was no wind

In those days we did not have leashes
Or ropes for our children in airports
We skipped along behind them

No runway or landing pad
No nursery or laboratory
No public or private school

Would ever be able to hold him
It was like giving a tropical storm
Some time out on land

It was as if a TV show ran constantly
In his mind the innocent kid
Kept breaking out of prison

✦

He was a little Bartleby
Of the nursery he despised kindergarten
And preferred not to

He clung to the couch he held fast
To the chair we dragged him out
Of the closet kicking and screaming

For an after-school ritual he rushed around
The house turning over furniture
And throwing books at the wall

He pushed over a lamp and tossed pillows
Through the door he nearly broke down
He kicked out the window twice

He had a fit on the front lawn
In the driveway in a friend's house
He locked himself in the bathroom

He started yelling at the referee
And stomped off the field in a fury
It was a bad call

He wanted he needed to buy something
Every day a new video system an iguana
A baseball bat a football helmet

He wanted he needed to go right away
To the arcade in the Galleria
Where you won tokens that brought rewards

Someone told us he had King's Syndrome
He thought he was royalty
And everyone should treat him like a king

We understood the desperation of the therapist
Who locked the door and sat on him
When he tried to leave the room

◆

The sun is tired
And so I'm hoisting him up
And carrying him on my shoulders

Over the hill or through the park
Around the pond back to the car
Home from the ballgame

He's scrambling up my back
His bare legs tightening
Around my neck

I'm grasping his ankles
Giving him a seat in the grandstands
Just above my head

The sun wants to see
The stage over the crowd
And look down upon the world

He's bounding onto my shoulders
In the swimming pool
And diving off

I can still feel his slippery feet
Why is he so scalding
Hot on my shoulders

I'm lifting him over my back
And striding through the woods
Like a tree walking with an orb

Branching out of its trunk
He's perched atop my ladder
At the fireworks display

But he's restless
And wants to bolt
I didn't come here to watch the fireworks

♦

I remember the five-year-old collector
Who started with four samurai slammers
Teens with attitude

He liked the way ordinary kids
Morphed into Rangers and piloted Zords
Deprogrammed from the dark side

I remember the boy who needed Beanie Babies
And then graduated to Transformers
Comic books and anime cards

Magic cards we called *cardboard crack*
I remember the collector who liked the hit
Of buying or selling it didn't matter what

He sold lemonade and cookies
And handmade paintings
Hastily brushed

Which he hawked for a dollar apiece
In front of the Menil Collection
Across the street from our house

Maybe someday little boy
Your work will be hanging
Inside the museum visitors said

While the artist just smiled
And nodded
And took their money

I remember the boy who never cared
What he bought or sold after he bought
Or sold it it's all over now

He loved cartoons where nothing is final
Everyone gets flattened and then gets up
And starts running around again

✦

He did not like to remember
His tics were always worse
When it was hot

He did not like to remember
Wiping his face like a third-base coach
Giving signals to the batter

He did not like to remember
Days of obsessive eye blinking
Nights of touching his hair

For a while he developed
A heavy sniff almost a snort
People moved away from us in theaters

He did not like to remember
His tantrums at school after school
They did not get along

He did not like to remember
Teachers and therapists
Tests he did not want to take

He did not like to remember
Drugs that made him lazy and fat
They overmedicate kids now

He told anyone who would listen
He'd rather buy a stogie
Drink a beer smoke a joint

He did not like to remember
His diagnosis for Tourette syndrome
Or pervasive developmental disorder

Not otherwise specified
He knew something was wrong
He did not like to remember

✦

The population of his feelings
Could not be governed
By the authorities

He had reasons why
Reason disobeyed him
And voted him out of office

Anxiety
His constant companion
Made it difficult to rest

Unruly party of one
Forget about truces or compromises
The barricades will be stormed

Every day was an emergency
Every day called for another emergency
Meeting of the cabinet

In his country
There were scenes
Of spectacular carnage

Hurricanes welcomed him
He adored typhoons and tornadoes
Furies unleashed

Houses lifted up
And carried to the sea
Uncontained uncontainable

Unbolt the doors
Fling open the gates
Here he comes

Chaotic wind of the gods
He was trouble
But he was our trouble

✦

Rainer Maria Rilke sacrificed everything
For his art he dedicated himself
To the Great Work

I admired his single-mindedness
All through my twenties
I argued his case

Now I think he was a jerk
For skipping his daughter's wedding
For fear of losing his focus

He believed in the ancient enmity
Between daily life and the highest work
Or Ruth and the *Duino Elegies*

It is probably a middle-class prejudice
Of mine to think that Anna Akhmatova
Should have raised her son Lev

Instead of dumping him on her husband's mom
Motherhood is a bright torture she confessed
I was not worthy of it

Lev never considered it sufficient
For her to stand outside his prison
Month after month clutching packages

And composing *Requiem* for the masses
I argued with Rilke and Akhmatova
All the years I shuttled Gabriel to school

And then locked down with their poems
I argued with them while I scribbled away
In the pizza joints and video arcades

It is a true error to marry with poets
John Berryman concluded
Or to be by them

◆

He's singing the Poe Elementary School blues
He's singing the Shlenker School blues a day school
For the offspring of upper-middle-class strivers

He's singing the Montessori School blues
He's singing the Monarch School blues
For kids with executive function disorders

I give you the educational consultant blues
One lived in San Antonio one in Idaho
He's singing the Little Keswick blues

A therapeutic boarding school in central Virginia
Where many drive up and say it feels like home
It did not feel like home to us

He's singing the Devereux Glenholme blues
Where they searched boys for contraband
And treated chewing gum like shooting heroin

He's singing the Franklin Academy blues
Where nonverbal learning disabilities are
Overcome and everyone heads off to college

He's singing the five Quint two Intercession blues
The transitions that could not be made
The dreaded summonses

I give you the no-mercy rule
The let's-get-thrown-out-of-school-
And-hire-tutors-to-graduate-from-home blues

He's singing the Dubspot blues
The fantasy of Reason and Record
The electronic-music-has-died blues

There are no more academies to attend
He was not befriended by study
A therapist called him one of the lost boys

◆

For his eighteenth birthday
As a special present to himself
He took himself off all medications

All those drug regimens for tics and tantrums
For disorders that were being named
By the month and year

Obsessive-compulsive disorder
Mood disorder
Oppositional-defiant disorder

Attention deficit hyperactivity disorder
Combined type and bipolar disorder
Mixed type also dyslexia dysgraphia

For a while we were on the Autism spectrum
But then PDD-NOS was dropped
As a diagnosis for the new manual

All those special cocktails
All those weekly appointments
And adjustments by the doctors

Someone had to keep track
Of the side effects of taking clonidine
Adderall Depakote Ritalin

Strattera Abilify Concerta
Levoxyl Paxil and Trileptal
In the morning and at bedtime

Risperdal the special culprit
I fought against and lost
The argument lasted for years

He hated the way it puffed his face
And ballooned his body sixty pounds
He pleaded for drug holidays

✦

The evening with its lamps burning
The night with its head in its hands
The early morning

I look back at the worried parents
Wandering through the house
What are we going to do

The evening of the clinical
The night of the psychological
The morning facedown in the pillow

The experts can handle him
The experts have no idea
How to handle him

There are enigmas in darkness
There are mysteries
Sent out without searchlights

The stars are hiding tonight
The moon is cold and stony
Behind the clouds

Nights without seeing
Mornings of the long view
It's not a sprint but a marathon

Whatever we can do
We must do
Every morning's resolve

But sometimes we suspected
He was being punished
For something obscure we had done

I would never abandon the puzzle
Sleeping in the next room
But I could not solve it

✦

Fatherhood could not be conquered
My friend Donald concluded
It could be *turned down* in his generation

I dialed it down and let Janet deal
With the medical doctors the various
Specialists who plagued us with help

The psychologists the psychiatrists
The neuropsychiatrists the speech therapists
The art therapists the occupational therapists

Have I left anyone out what about
The head of the Movement Disorders Center
Who told us he had two thousand patients

In the seventies I was one of the fools
Who took the side of nurture versus nature
I thought sociobiology was a crock

Think of the brain as a switchboard
Dr. B. said stiffly
He has a lot of things knocked out

I didn't want to I couldn't help it
I pictured a system of circuits misfiring
Wires crossed and darkened

He is going to continue to develop
All through his twenties he explained
He's going to be thirty before you know

It was good news it was hopeful
But it made me think of the celebration
When everyone jammed into the dining room

For the giant cake with my picture on it
And I watched all my friends
Eating pieces of my face

✦

And the Father the Law
Who should have been handing down
Commandments from on high

What was he doing all those years
When he should have been reassuring his wife
And taking charge of his son

What was he doing when he should have been
Standing fast and overruling the experts
Who were guessing what to do

He should have been teaching him
Character teaching him values teaching him
To become the man he was meant to become

What was he doing the Father the Law
In the exact middle of life
But fighting for his vocation

Ghost of my earlier self
I see you muttering to yourself
And pacing up and down

In a room on the second floor
Of the house all night every night
Through your late forties

What were you seeking but escape
The transport and the despondency
Of the old makers

Poet who labored so hard at your craft
On a scarred wooden desk
It is late now

It is time
To turn off the lamp
And come down from your study

◆

After we moved to New York
I asked him if he was lonely at school
And he said *I'm used to it Dad*

He wanted to come home to the city
With attention deficit disorder
Where he was less lonely

He found his natural habitat
In the dense forest of buildings
Hovering over the stores of Manhattan

He wore baggy shorts and a bold t-shirt
If the music is too loud you're too old
And sang along to his headset on Broadway

Every now and then he glanced back at me
A middle-aged father weaving
Through traffic behind him

Sometimes he paused for me
To catch up to buy him cologne
Or two pairs of sunglasses for ten bucks

He liked designer knockoffs
And rolled along incognito
Among the derelicts and crazies

He was a fifteen-year-old in the city
No more no less
But I imagined him as a colorful unnamed bird

Warbling his difference from the robins and sparrows
And scissoring past the vendors on every corner
I kept thinking of him as a wild fledgling

Who tilted precariously on one wing
And peered back at me from the sudden height
Before disappearing over the treetops

◆

Take the lamp out of the mud
By the side of the road
Uncover the drum

The torch has sputtered
On its side in the rain
Light it again

Take it down to the corner
Where a group of boys grows
In the dark like a garden

He met them fooling around on Broadway
They thought it was funny
The way he'd say anything to anyone

The group invited him to hang out
It started with Kevin Tristan and Danny
Who nicknamed himself *Big Bird*

They introduced him to D.
Meaty and large slow-moving slow-talking
Who once stayed with us for a month

J.M. came by sometimes a con man
Who looked like a model he said
He was born in Israel or the Dominican Republic

Then he met Joe the center
The straw-haired chosen one
Update Freddie Mercury from Queen

Tune up the rage
For the speed-metal band
Swaggering down the street

Take the lamp the drum
The torch lofted up and carried
Through the middle of town

◆

Mr. Impulsive walked out of class
When he did not like what the teacher said
It was boring

Mr. Impulsive scurried out in a storm
Wearing shorts and a wife beater
Soon he was shivering

The neighbors complained to the landlord
Complained to me but Mr. Impulsive
Could not be bothered to close the gate

Mr. Impulsive left the house without his keys
I don't know how many times
He camped out on the front stoop

One night he convinced a neighbor
To shimmy the lock with a credit card
He was never locked out again

Mr. Impulsive will not be sleeping at home
He'd rather stay out and crash
Wherever he finds himself at five a.m.

He could be oddly well-mannered
To the parents of his friends
He was usually welcome

From the notebook of Mr. Impulsive
It is better to sneak through a side door
Than to wait in line like a sucker

It is not necessary to get directions
It's much better to head out right now
Time doesn't matter

These were the antics of Mr. Impulsive
Who never knew where he was going
Until he got there

◆

From the Book of Teenage Rage
It's just a transitional stage they said
He was depressed defiant lethargic rude

Restless and defensive he shuttled back and forth
Between the Upper West Side and Brooklyn
His parents were getting divorced

He told people that he was sick of school
That's why he had gotten thrown out on purpose
He wanted to come home instead

When he dyed his hair red blond and green
It was as if he'd been running through
The spectrum of the rainbow

When he colored his hair blue
The sink was covered with blue dye
As if the sky was turned upside down in a bowl

Lights turned on all over the house
Air conditioners blasting two TVs blaring
Cabinet doors should not be closed

Upstairs in his room half-eaten plates of food
Open take-out containers uncapped drinks
Stained sheets clothes strewn on the floor

One toilet clogged the other plunged
Wet towels piled on the floor
He forgot to walk the dog

He was too exhausted
He could not be expected to answer
When the tutor rang the bell

When he read Cliffs Notes
For *Catcher in the Rye* he thought
Holden Caulfield was boring

✦

A teenage boy finds himself
Lying facedown on top of a bus
Racing through a tunnel out of the city

He is plastered to the slippery roof
And breathing in the terrible fumes
Which go on for miles and miles

A boy clinging to the surface
His mouth full of dust
His arms and legs spread-eagled

A winged angel in the grime
Remembers the ocean wind
The spray in his face the fog lifting

The bus slows in heavy traffic
And the boy peers down to see
Himself in the front seat

Of a passing car a stick figure
Crayoned between his parents
And then the bus picks up speed

And flies into the faceless darkness
And the boy and his parents
Become a vanishing scrawl

Lying facedown on top of a bus
Racing through a tunnel out of the city
A teenage boy finds himself

Plastered to the slippery roof
And breathing in the exhaust
The darkness visible at last

And then suddenly a blackbird
Floating like charred paper
The bruised blue sky

✦

Maybe I shouldn't go on talking
About the self-involved young social worker
Who convinced everyone

She could handle Gabriel on her own
In Amherst where she inherited a house
From her estranged parents

It takes a village I said
She could not manage him
But he settled into her basement anyway

It took two months for her
To decide to sell her house and move
Into a smaller place without him

She sent me an e-mail explaining
That it was just too taxing to live with him
But he was ready to stay by himself

And she could check on him weekly
For one hundred dollars per hour
They could shop together

Maybe I shouldn't go on talking
About an undertrained overwhelmed
Unprofessional twenty-eight-year-old

But on his third night in a new place
He felt a terrible stabbing pain in his chest
And walked to the police station in his pajamas

The ambulance took him to the hospital
But the doctors couldn't find anything wrong
With his heart it was a panic attack

Laurie and I came up with a plan
For a system of mentor/companions
And he never suffered another one again

♦

I'd like to raise a glass to Cliff
Bearded social worker mud-man potter
Who shambled up for an interview

And worked with Gabriel for two years
In Amherst no one made more progress
Gabe condescended to him at first

Because he was really a hick poor guy
Only New Yorkers had everything figured out
And the rest of the world was playing catch-up

I'd like to raise a glass to Moises and Christa
The Brazilian psychologist the substitute teacher
And New Age mother who companioned him

I'd like to raise a glass to Tim
Founder of YES
Who called him *a bright spark of a person*

And taught him the rights of the disabled
Let's also save a glass for Melissa
Who found him three jobs through WEYA

Summer of Amherst Department of Public Works
Summer of Meals on Wheels
And Forbes Public Library in Northampton

He learned to drive and got his license
I thought he was too out of control to own
A car Janet bought him one anyway

He earned three college credits for a class
In marketing at Holyoke Community College
He believed he could sell anything at all

I'd like to raise a toast to anyone
Who can convince me there is a world out there
Where he is selling something to someone

✦

From the storybook of bluster
And bad judgment
From the annals of loneliness

From the history of kids he met
On the street in special programs
It was dangerous to stay in Amherst

Lord of Misadventure
I'm scared of rounding him up
And turning him into a story

God of Scribbles and Erasures
I hope he shines through
Like a Giacometti portrait

I keep scraping the canvas
And painting him over again
But he keeps slipping away

He was like a spider
Preyed on by other spiders
And older insects

Sweet venom
His arrivals were swift
And his departures sudden

I couldn't understand how
He lifted the shower door
Right off its hinges

When Gabriel cooked
The flames rose too high
And the fire alarm sounded

When the fire alarm sounded
He tore it off the wall
And left the wires dangling

✦

From the Book of Regrets
Maybe we should have gone to Tokyo
We almost visited once

At the time of the Pokémon craze
A bunch of kids in Japan suffered
Epileptic seizures like his

Maybe we should have tried Edinburgh
Or Dublin to see if we felt at home
He decided he was Scots-Irish

We never heard a nightingale
Or played cricket on the beach
Or sang karaoke together

Maybe we should have kept him home
From boarding school Janet and I
Never quit arguing about it

I should have been calmer
I should have been more patient
At least I never whacked him

Though I wanted to a couple of times
The only punishment that ever worked
Was leaving the room

Maybe we were too hard on him
Maybe we were too soft
The therapist recommended

I kick him out on the street
I never had the stomach for it
Maybe I should have forced him

Into a wilderness program but how
He would have hated it hated me
Though maybe he'd be alive

✦

It was a mistake
To put her daughter in an orphanage
During the Moscow famine

Tsvetaeva realized too late
It was an error
That could never be rectified

And cost her a daughter
Who starved to death she said
God punished me

It was a mistake
To marry off his darling second
Daughter at ten-and-a-half

Tagore wrote *The Child* for Rani
On her deathbed at thirteen
It could not assuage his guilt

He returned to the Grief House
For his youngest son his eldest daughter
Tears could not assuage his guilt

When Ungaretti lost his nine-year-old boy
He understood that death is death
In an extremely brutal way

It was the most terrible event of my life
I know what death means
I knew it even before

But when the best part of me was ripped away
I experienced death in myself
From that moment on

It would strike me as shameless
To talk about it
That pain will never stop tormenting me

✦

Adolescents in the city
Of noise young men
In the land of confusion

Gabriel called him *Broseph*
Joe called him *Hebro*
Laurie called it a *bromance*

Broseph liked rock and roll old-style
Hebro liked emo-punk
Stomp to the music

They smoked weed and watched ballgames
Got into everything with everyone
Hustled girls everywhere

They got the call for the rave
Subwayed it out to Williamsburg
Banged around clubs

Gabriel came home with a skinny Russian
Model who sat there mutely
And refused to eat

She skipped out on him once
When he was down with a cold
No no man you've got it all wrong

Joe explained in the restaurant
We don't need relationships
What we need are relations

Often they argued about one thing or another
It was all very Shakespearean Joe said
Gabe was my dude my equal

Me and Gabe were young men together
Whenever I did my endeavors
Gabe was with me

✦

We took him to Arlington Park racetrack
But they wouldn't let him in the clubhouse
Because he was wearing a t-shirt and jeans

He disappeared
And in ten minutes he came back wearing
A button-down a tie and a blue blazer

He stopped by with a dozen incense candles
You don't even like incense Laurie said
It didn't matter he had gotten them for free

He bought ten cheeseburgers for ten bucks
On the dollar menu at McDonald's
And threw six of them away

He brought a six-pack of beer
Into the common room of the nursing home
To watch a football game with my mother

Because everyone needs a good beer
Especially the guy on the ventilator
And the nurses who work too hard

He said the countryside
Made him feel nervous he wanted
A twenty-four-hour kind of city

He woke me up at two a.m.
To take a walk he needed to talk
Laurie pulled me back into bed

He had flat feet and an awkward gait
He didn't like to dance he liked
To go to raves and chill with friends

He couldn't pay attention
But his meds made him feel sleepy
And he sold them to college kids

✦

He liked to kick back and remember
The time we were riding home
In a taxicab on the West Side Highway

And my mother offered to take him
To a strip club for his twenty-first birthday
What's wrong with that she wanted to know

Why they couldn't celebrate together
That's just what you want he bellowed
Going for a lap dance with Grandma

He liked to kick back and declare
He wanted to track down his birth mother
To see if he really had Celtic blood

He liked to kick back and tell my family
About the time he saw an American Hasidic
Jewish reggae musician at Hampshire College

He saw Nicholas Cage going up an escalator
In a movie theater and turned to his friends
I hate Nicholas Cage he has such a big head

He liked to kick back and tell us
How much he liked weed and 'shrooms
How bad could it be for you he said

It comes out of the ground
He liked to kick back and roll a spliff
With his friends at night

He always liked to go higher and higher
We're here he'd say lifting his hand
To the middle of his chest

But we need to go here
He continued on
And raised his hand up to his neck

✦

Friedrich Rückert wrote 425 poems
After his two youngest children
Died from scarlet fever

Within sixteen days of each other
In 1833 and 1834 he could not cope
And often thought they had gone out

For a while *they'll be home soon*
He told himself to tell his wife
They're only taking a long walk

Mahler scored five of those poems
In 1901 and 1904 for a vocalist
And an orchestra to break your heart

As soon as I heard the plaintive oboe
And the descending movement of the horn
And the lyric baritone entering

I felt I should not be listening
To Dietrich Fischer-Dieskau singing
Kindertotenlieder with the Berlin Philharmonic

Mahler's wife was superstitious
And thought he was chancing disaster
With *Songs on the Death of Children*

Now the sun wants to rise so brightly
As if nothing terrible had happened overnight
The tragedy happened to me alone

Mahler knew he could never have written them
After his four-year-old daughter died
From scarlet fever three years later

He said he felt sorry for himself
That he needed to write these songs
And for the world that would listen to them

✦

Mallarmé was left in fragments
And could not right it
After his adored Anatole

His exquisite second born
His future prospects
A celestial soul

Succumbed to rheumatic fever
Treacherous blow of death
Ridiculous enemy

Ailing in springtime
Mourned in winter
His eight-year-old was lodged

In a little cemetery
Overlooking the Seine
Where skaters glided by at Christmas

And barges froze in the canals
And the moon eclipsed
His future projects

Hugo could speak of his daughter's death
Hugo was happy to be able to speak
Of his daughter's death

But it was impossible for Mallarmé
Though year after year
He labored at a tomb for Anatole

Which he could never complete
An immortality made human
An offering to the absolute

With his son
Transposed by death
Mallarmé was left with fragments

✦

He came by my office for cash
Every Monday Wednesday and Friday
I was good for thirty bucks a pop sometimes more

You only drop by when you want your money
I said but he protested *it's not like that Dad*
He didn't like to think of himself that way

I was usually working at the computer
When he strolled in
Dad you're the sort of person

Who needs to work a lot
I'm the sort of person
Who needs a lot of down time

He wasn't doing anything all day long
He just slept in and hung with his friends
And so I tried to convince him to volunteer

For an organization he was contemptuous
He thought volunteering was for stooges
He didn't like charities either

He told his friends he had once
Attended a six-month training program
In audio production at EWF

He had some skills using Pro Tools
And Reason software he had major skills
In DJing and music production

He told my friends he was going back to school
To finish up his degree in marketing
At the University of Massachusetts

He just needed a few more credits
To collect his diploma
Maybe next summer

❖

From the playbook
Say you get caught lifting eighty bucks
Out of your dad's wallet or your mom's purse

Simply deny it deny everything
Never take responsibility for what
You could not possibly have done

The strategy for getting what you want
When you want it is simple
Never take *no* for an answer

Pump up the volume
Remember that *no* is not an option
It is just a temporary setback

He wanted us to buy him a bicycle
So he could deliver specialty donuts and ice cream
Concoctions at night in Hell's Kitchen

It was a scheme we refused
He found an old girl's bicycle on the side
Of the street and fixed it up for twenty bucks

Take that parents
He never used the bike because the shop
Didn't bother to call him back Janet still has it

He was determined to get his own apartment
And certain that epilepsy qualified him
For a free apartment from the city

Otherwise he could move in with Tamar
Her dad would get her an apartment as soon
As she went back to school full time

He was finally accepted for Job Path
He could make some real dough at last
And get an apartment after Labor Day

◆

I stood at the damaged site
Across the street from my house
And watched a steel ball

Crashing into the homeless shelter
Abandoned on Dean Street
All the people scattered

It takes tremendous force
To weaken a building
And turn bricks into rubble

It doesn't take long
The crane swung around
And pitched the heavy ball

Into the guts of the structure
Holding its side
Like a wounded veteran

The hard hats gathered
To watch the pendulum swing
Into the concrete body

Of a building slated for demolition
So there could be progress
I was against the project

And riveted to the wreckage
Time and again the fighter wavered
And finally collapsed

I did not stay to see the building
Broken down into debris
And then carted away

Some nights I could not tell
If he was the wrecking ball
Or the building it crashed into

◆

It's the way he roared into the house
And started to rant
Against those he did not like

Rude waiters who charged him extra
For stuff he ordered too much
On a whim his appetite vanished

He did not like certain cousins
Preppies fake bohemians in the Village
Spoiled Amherst students *Mass-holes*

Especially bugged him
Social workers he did not like
Men in tight leggings feminists

Do you even know what a feminist is
Laurie asked him he did not
Like hairy-armed lesbians kissing

On the street in Northampton
All right all right that's enough now
I said it was hard to calm him down

Once he started to rail
Against boy bands or Hasidic Jews
Or boarding schools those hellholes

Models and snobs annoyed him
He didn't have much use
For bullies or honor students

Don't be a hater his friends said
Don't drink a pitcher of Haterade
But he just laughed

And continued the blast
His parents did not escape his wrath
I wonder if he forgave us

◆

Laurie and I looked around
Jittery and shaken the after-draft
Was like drinking a pot of coffee

And then trying to sleep
It was impossible
To keep track of him at all hours

He spent whatever money he had
Whenever he had it spendthrift gambler
I could never stay mad at him for long

He just shrugged his shoulders
And laughed helplessly
I couldn't help it I had to Dad

He wasn't made for a world
Of checkbooks and savings accounts
Stockbrokers investment bankers

Charlie called him *a Clown of God*
He wasn't *a Monster of Subtlety*
Like the two of us

He would try anything once he hazarded
He was sometimes scared
He was never scared enough

Of scoundrels and drug dealers
He thought teachers and supervisors
And psychiatrists were the enemy

Policemen riled him he had rights
A lover a posse of friends
No one could restrain him

King of the Sudden Impulse
Lord of the Torrent
Emperor of the Impetuous

♦

He breezed into the office
With his girlfriend and hit me up
For extra money because of the storm

Pounding across the Atlantic Ocean
He was heading to the store to buy food
So they wouldn't starve to death ha ha

Love you he coughed and kissed me
See you next week he was out
The door like a thousand other times

Some people were nervous others festive
When we closed for the day
And told everyone to buy supplies

Is this the apocalypse line
Somebody asked the disorderly crowd
Outside the hardware store on First Avenue

The apocalypse line was getting longer
We should forget about power downtown
The spokesman for Con Ed said

When Hurricane Irene hit North Carolina
And started to churn up the East Coast
The city decided to evacuate

370,000 people from the low-lying areas
Of Manhattan my friends in Zone A
Boarded their windows and stormed out

On the local news I watched some idiots
Sitting on the beach and working
On their tans in Asbury Park

Here comes Irene bearing down on us
It's time to get out
Of the apocalypse line

✦

He left the house during a rainstorm
Almost impulsively
He rushed out headlong into the night

While everyone else hunkered down
With flashlights and batteries
The city on high alert

The subways closing down
Stay home the mayor said
And only go out in an emergency

But he left the house during a rainstorm
And never came home
Where was he going in such a hurry

It was almost as if the hurricane
Swept him away in a flood
Swarming over the banks

He left the house
And headed to another town
We had no idea where he had gone

He was a secret
We could not decipher
And no one would help us find him

We called to report him missing
No one would help us find him
For four days and four nights

We tried desperately to track him down
The hurricane carried him away
He rushed out headlong into the night

And I never saw him alive again
Most reckless of reckless angels
Who left the house during a rainstorm

♦

I was at home in Brooklyn
Working on a lyric
About the troubadours

When he left the apartment
On the Upper West Side
Looking for an adventure

I was reading the eleven poems
Of Guilhem IX Duke of Aquitane
The earliest troubadour

When he left his girlfriend
And his mother at home
To meet a friend for a drink

He said he would be home soon
Don't worry about anything
He texted Tamar

I didn't know he had gone out
In the rain it was raining steadily
I was at home in Brooklyn working

On a simple poem about nothing
A troubadour song
How nothing came to me

When he took the train to Jersey City
If that's how he got there
I thought he was at home

While I worked on a song
About nothing
And then went to sleep

Without knowing anything
I startled awake in the morning
I woke up and he was missing

♦

We kept calling his phone
It went straight to voicemail
This is Gabe leave a message

We called 311
We called 911 every day
The police refused to help us

We begged them to help they refused
Because he wasn't under sixteen or over sixty-five
He didn't have a life-threatening illness

They said that epilepsy doesn't count
It's not that dangerous
They had never heard of his disorder

This happens a lot with twenty-two-year-olds
They said he was probably just hanging out
With the wrong crowd

He hadn't been arrested he wasn't
In the hospitals we thought
Maybe he was stranded somewhere

And couldn't get home
The trains had stopped running
Maybe he had spent all his money

And couldn't call us his phone
Needed to be charged
This is Gabe leave a message

We said he had never disappeared before
We said he always called home
We said he had a developmental disorder

It didn't matter his disabilities
Were not on the list
And so the police refused to help us

✦

He never liked it when things closed
It gave him the feeling of being locked
In a room with bars on the windows

He never liked it when the weather
Interfered with plans he hadn't made yet
He was never too sick to go out

When he was ten years old I had to drag him
Out of the swimming pool in a deluge
He wanted to cannonball off the diving board

He wanted to stop and slash some golf balls
He wanted to soap up the wet car
And let the sky wash it down

I remember the morning we escaped
From Galveston just before the hurricane
We coasted in front of the destruction

One night I came out of a restaurant
In a light rain and started to drive home
But the storm dropped so suddenly

I turned out of the driveway
Into a waist-high wall of water
And floated the car to the side of the road

I sloshed home through the flood
It took over an hour Gabriel shouted
That car is dead in the water

I thought I was the sort of person
Who could get pummeled by a storm
And stagger home to laugh about it

Forget about the 468 subway stations
Wind shut down the Staten Island Ferry
The bridges and tunnels were closed

✦

I couldn't sleep I never could sleep
I just stared out the window
Into the blankest space

Not thinking exactly
Worrying obsessively
Waiting for daylight

I left the house at five thirty a.m.
And wandered past the drunks
Sprawled out on Flatbush Avenue

I crossed the Manhattan Bridge
Hooded with blue shadows
The first bicyclists of the morning

I picked my way through Chinatown
Thick with fruit stands
And born-again commuters

I steered my way up Bowery
Sliding from Skid Row
Into respectability

I moved past Canal and Delancey
The New Museum the Bowery Poetry Club
The Bowery Mission Cooper Union

I saw people buying coffee from trucks
And ordering breakfast in diners
Exactly as if nothing had happened

Who cares I ended up at my desk
In an office building in midtown
Wondering what I was going to do

All day the subways were running again
The city presumed normal
My son still missing

✦

Joe thought that Gabriel was shacked up
With a Brazilian woman he'd met
A couple of times in TriBeCa

He didn't know her name he just called her
Brazil all their friends did he said
He had only been to her pad

Two or three times he could remember it
Because it was next door to a club
Maybe on Worth or White Street

We found it after a couple of tries
She lived on the second floor
With a recording studio in the front

We rang the buzzer
For every apartment in the building
No one was home in the early evening

We decided to go across the street
To sit on a stoop and stake out
Five floors of empty apartments

They looked comatose in the looming dark
Suddenly the streetlamp across the way
Began to flicker on and off

It's a sign Joe said *I hope it doesn't
Go out* he was very agitated
It's just a streetlamp I told him

The light wavered for a moment
And then flicked off for good
I don't know where Gabe is

Joe said despondently *he's lost*
And that's when he knew
His friend's life had been extinguished

✦

Gabriel made his last phone call
To a number in Jersey City
Janet and I decided to go there

It was just a subway ride away
We were probably wasting our time
But why not do something else to find him

We took a train ride and a cab
To the West District Precinct
On Communipaw Avenue

We marched up to the desk
And told our story to the clerk
Who requested our driver's licenses

We sat on cheap chairs in the lobby
And wondered what we were doing
In a cruddy police station in Jersey City

We waited for twenty minutes
For forty-five minutes an hour passed
Why had we decided to go there

The sergeant is investigating it
We were told to keep waiting
What else could we do

We had been waiting for four days
We had a disease no one wanted
To help us it could never be cured

Four men came out to talk to us
And we followed them up the stairs
Into an office where one of them said

We have some bad news for you
Your son Gabriel has passed away
We're sorry for your loss

✦

Something about Craig's List
Alcohol a drug called GHB
Someone called an ambulance

Something about emergency technicians
Who hooked him up to an IV
And tried to revive him

Something about his pallor
Skin cool to the touch
Pupils fixed and dilated

Something about Jersey City Medical Center
Where he was seen immediately
He didn't have a pulse he wasn't breathing

On Saturday morning his heart stopped
He never woke up again
He died of cardiac arrest at 6:08

Something about an autopsy
Respectful of Jewish law
To determine the cause of death

Something about finding a funeral home
His body delivered from Newark
And a place to bury him

Something about a ride to the train station
A pledge to the grieving parents
A rabbi to conduct the service

Something about amputating your arm
Because it bothered you
It was never a wing anyway

Something about amputating your leg
Because it hurts
You will never walk away from this

✦

What was done by the twenty-two-year-old
Who took an odorless colorless liquid
On a rainy night in late August

Cannot be undone by the paramedics
Or the doctors or the officers
Working the night shift

What was taken cannot be untaken
By the kid who took a ride out
To Mallory Street in Jersey City

And dropped a cap of GHB
For a long powerless ride to the end
Of a night that would never end

I had never heard of his killer
Synthesized in clandestine labs
And sold for twenty bucks a tab

I had never heard of *Liquid Ecstasy*
Georgia Home Boy Goop Easy Lay
Grievous Bodily Harm

What made him feel drowsy
And euphoric what relaxed him
Into a kind of stupor

What made him feel affectionate
And sociable what induced nausea
And made it impossible to breathe

What caused a seizure caused a coma
What stopped his heart and left him
Lifeless on the floor

I will never know why it was written
What was taken cannot be untaken
What was done cannot be undone

✦

Like a blind wing turning in the dark
Like a lunatic spark of light
In the thickening clouds

Like a flashlight flickering in the woods
A broken flashlight in the dark
It will never be fixed again

Like a lighthouse on the horizon
An abandoned lighthouse
Its beacon wandering at sea

Like a crescent snuffed out
In a storm over the waves
The drowned moon

It should have been an eagle
Cutting through the fog
It should have been a swallow

I once saw a car careening
Into a streetlamp on the corner
Its headlights crushed

Like the sound of a stone crashing
Into a wall in a deserted neighborhood
It was too late to save the stone or the wall

Like a stone shot out of a slingshot
In the dead of night in the dark
The slingshot could not control the stone

The thunder sounded like a machine gun
In the dark sky it rattled and stopped
The lightning flashed and died

I was asleep at 6:08 on Saturday morning
I did not see the flashing light
I did not hear the roar

✦

It rained for twenty-two years
And two hundred and forty days
All the days and nights of his life

The rain it raineth every day
From the midnight of his birth
To the early morning of his death

A light rain fell across New Orleans
On the day he entered the world
Before the great flood

Torrential rains swelled the Tiber in Rome
And overflowed the bayous in Houston
We once drove across a bridge of rain

Heavy rains pounded the fields
Of central Virginia the roads of Connecticut
Telephone wires wavered in the wind

His apartment flooded in Massachusetts
He walked through a hallway of water
And stomped into town

The roads were sleek with rain and sleet
But he drove to New York at three a.m.
He skidded home traffic was light

The rain in the city did not deter him
He splashed through the downpour
And bolted the house in a rainstorm

In New York City the rain was constant
For days in Jersey City it never stopped
I can't bear to think of him in the wet ground

He will come down like rain
Upon the mown grass
As showers that water the earth

♦

Like a swimmer strolling into the ocean
On a breezy day it seems fine
Suddenly the waves start carrying him away

He was always a good swimmer
No need to pay attention to the warning
Flags on a day without lifeguards

Now he can't get back to shore
Panic begins as a flutter in his legs
And then blasts through his chest

He is fighting against the waves
Riptides drag him down
And swarm him into the underworld

He was somebody's errant boy
Somebody taught him the crawl stroke
Somebody taught him to respect the water

He stripped off his clothes
And dropped them in a pile on the shore
His last effects

Like a swimmer strolling into the ocean
On an unsuspecting day
No one knew he was out there

Swimming in the rain
The waves got higher and higher
And slashed the shore

He left without a care don't worry
He was a strong swimmer
But the ocean was stronger

His last fight against the waves
Riptides dragged him down
And swarmed him into the underworld

◆

The stone says nothing
The stone remembers nothing
An ordinary stone

It just sits there coldly in the dirt
By the fence in the cemetery
Doing nothing

All day long all night long
The stone never moves never knows
No one thinks about it

The stone cannot know
No one can forget about it
Because no one knows it is there

We stood at the grave site
Studying the view from the grounds
It's just far enough from the road

We stood in the low grass
And marched around the trees
And made a final decision

The stone knew nothing about anything
Until someone picked it up
And turned it into a memorial stone

The stone was singled out
It could have been a weapon
Someone could have tossed it

Away without a care
But instead someone picked it up
And laid it gently down

At Section 3 Row R Grave 12
Rest in peace at last hyperactive one
I will stand above you aghast

◆

The Regional Medical Examiner a doctor
Conducted an external examination
Followed by an autopsy

On the unembalmed refrigerated body
Identified as Gabriel Hirsch
Case #09110776

The body is clad in the following items
T-shirt with a design cut
One pair of boxer shorts cut

Accompanying the body
One multi-colored wallet with a Visa Debit card
One Metro card one Massachusetts driver's license

The body is of a well-developed well-nourished
Average frame 182 pounds 70 inches
White male

The nose and facial bones are palpably intact
The trachea is in the midline
The torso is unremarkable

There are no injuries
To his upper and lower extremities
His genitalia show a normal circumcised male

Postmortem Changes
There is moderate symmetrical rigor mortis
On the upper and lower extremities neck and jaw

Lividity is pink posterior and fixed
The body is cool
Subsequent to refrigeration

Evidence of Injuries
External and Internal
None

◆

His brain weighed 1530 grams
And had a glistening leptomeninges
The cerebral hemispheres were symmetrical

His heart weighed 380 grams
The left ventricular measured 1.3 cm
And the right measured 0.5 cm thick

His right lung weighed 1000 grams
His left lung weighed 700 grams
The bronchi were slightly hyperemic

His liver weighed 2130 grams
His gallbladder contained 8 ml
Of green viscus bile without stones

His spleen weighed 440 grams
There were no enlarged lymph nodes
The bone marrow was unremarkable

His right kidney weighed 180 grams
His left kidney weighed 190 grams
His bladder contained 250 ml of straw-colored urine

His stomach contained 20 ml of bloody fluid
His vermiform appendix was present
His small and large intestines were unremarkable

Specimens were submitted for histologic evaluation
Specimens were submitted for toxicological evaluation
There was no postmortem radiology

Sexual assault kit was made and prepared
DNA card prepared pulled scalp hair and fingerprints
Were taken and retained on file

Special consideration for autopsy was done
Without water all utensils and preparation were made
To remove and provide all blood or fluids back to the body

✦

He loved twisting rides on roller coasters
Coins fell from his pockets
When he was upside down

He loved tossing quarters into claw games
The noisy clang of slot machines
The soft light of casinos

He loved Nickel City in Northbrook
Twenty games for a buck he played
Four hundred games in an hour

I sat at the bar drinking a Diet Coke
And reading Apollinaire while he hurtled
From game to game in Dave & Buster's

He did not like family vacations in Wisconsin
That trip to Puerto Rico was a disaster
Thanksgiving in Texas did not elicit thanks

He loved Six Flags and Sea World
At Disneyworld he met the Ninja Turtles
I once took him to a Power Rangers concert

It surprised me how much he loved
Retracing Columbus's journey to the New World
On a high school field trip

He adored cruising back into Rome
And he condescended to me
Because I'd never been to Lisbon

He loved absinthe he said he drank it once
In Europe it tasted decadent
Like a girl who smelled of licorice and smoke

He loved the way the Mediterranean
Spread out and spanned the centuries
He loved to walk through the ruins

✦

He loved his 2000 green Acura Integra
Which he drove at high speeds
On deserted roads and winding highways

He loved pretending he could play the hi-hat
And crash cymbal like Travis Barker
The tattooed drummer for Blink-182

He loved the metal bands we heard
On Randall's Island in 2006
Disturbed Atreyu and Bad Acid Trip

He never gave up watching *Dragon Ball Z*
Pokémon and *Rocko's Modern Life*
He loved the moment in *The Boondock Saints*

When Murphy says *we're sorta like 7-Eleven*
We're not always doing business
But we're always open

He thought Massachusetts and Connecticut
Were boring states there was nothing
To do there he loved New York City

Something was always going on
He loved the Yankees and the Giants
He hated the Red Sox and the Patriots

He loved strong coffee specialty beers
Tamar's oatmeal cookies California burgers
Spicy Thai Indian and Mexican food

Dogs were his natural friends
He bet all his money on the long shot
At the racetrack he won big a couple of times

He loved his twenty-second birthday
Above all others it was the night of nights
Night of celebration

✦

Gabe was my best friend
Gabe was my right-hand man
Gabe was my wingman

I could tell you a lot of stories
I wrote them down we did everything
Together I think I'll drop it

And tell you what it felt like
To be with Gabe
On his twenty-second birthday

We went to a tattoo parlor
To watch an Ultimate Fighting match
On pay-per-view

We pooled four hundred bucks
And bet it on the underdog Cain Velasquez
Gabe said his head looks like a brick

We needed him to beat the UFC heavyweight champ
Brock Lesnar the baddest man on the planet
I once saw him pulverize a guy

I was nervous because everyone was shouting
About the killer in the octagon
And everything was on the line

But Gabe just gave me that little smirk
Of his you know the one I mean
It said we got this

That night we won big
We won really big
We pocketed eight hundred bucks

We danced on the tables
While others drank themselves under them
We painted the town red

✦

We bounced over to a club downtown
It was so crowded no one was getting in
But Gabe convinced the doorman

We were part of the wedding party
Just like in the movie Wedding Crashers
It was an after-party for a Chinese wedding

Gabe kept telling everyone
We were distant relatives of the bride and groom
We were just wearing our regular clothes

Jeans and t-shirts but Gabe was insistent
He had a baby face people wanted to believe him
Even when they knew he was lying

But once we got inside the party
The Chinese girls could barely speak English
And so we couldn't talk to them

We picked up Pepi too at the end of the night
We jumped on the backs of some monster
Garbage trucks to hitch a ride

The garbage men chased after us with baseball bats
But they were too fat to catch us
I can still hear them wheezing after us

We ended up at Union Square at dawn
Gabe headed off with his last forty bucks
Where are you going *I told him*

That's your last cash why don't you
Save some of it for tomorrow *but he said*
We've just had the night of our lives

And these homeless guys deserve a good breakfast
He bought two pies and twenty-four donuts
And handed them out to the homeless men in Union Square

✦

When I'm standing in line at the DMV
And the stoner next to me
Starts ranting about his parole officer

The dude has anger management issues
He's profiling me I couldn't get there
Because my grandmother was sick

When his buddy rolls into Big Nic's wearing
Cargo shorts and an Oscar the Grouch t-shirt
And I slip him a fifty-dollar bill

When one of his goofball friends swears
He will never take hard drugs again
And then drops three tabs of acid

And winds up in an institution in Tennessee
When I recite *Surprised by joy*
Impatient as the Wind

And think about Wordsworth's daughter Catherine
His six-year-old son Thomas his daughter Dora
Whose death caused him to quit

When someone's nephew someone's
Brother's oldest son a drunken teenager
Gets stuck on the railroad tracks

When I see fresh-faced soldiers
Hurrying off the plane in Atlanta
And everyone begins to clap

When the truck swerves into my lane
When lightning strikes a tree
While I am walking across a field

When the young anesthesiologist
Puts a needle into my arm
And I start to go under

✦

My friends studied him in high school
As the inventor of Polish poetry
A sixteenth-century humanist

Who translated the psalms into rhymed verse
And believed in meeting the world
With equanimity

But the poor bastard changed his mind
When Death swaddled up
His two-and-a-half-year-old daughter

I love him for calling on griefs
And laments from every quarter
O tears of Heraclitus O dirges of Simonides

To help him mourn the child
Whom Oblivion obliterated
With such uncanny force

We learned in school that funeral elegies
Laments and threnodies
Were reserved for big public occasions

And so the classical poets sang
Of heroes who fell valiantly in battle
Military leaders and philosopher-kings

But Kochanowski could not bear
To see his daughter's flowered dress
Her smooth ribbons her gold-clasped belt

And so he called on Urszula
To come back and haunt him again
As a shadow a dream or a ghost

Wisdom for me was castles in the air
I'm hurled like all the others
From the topmost stair

♦

Yamanoue worried that his son's soul
Would not know the right road
To take in the underworld

And so he offered to pay the fee
Of the courier from the realms below
To carry Furuhi on his back

A father broods that his son
Is wandering on the wrong road
Lost in the otherworld without a coat

I beseech you with offerings
Be true and lead him
On the straight road to heaven

Izumi could not understand
How her daughter could be cremated
And then vanish into the empty sky

When even the snow
The fragile white snow
Falls downward into this world

During the memorial service
She was distressed by the temple bell
That kept ringing and ringing

Listen to the resonance
Listen to the sound of longing
The sound of loss

Why did he have to keep striking
That holy bell for Naishi
Each strike was a blow

The grieving poets are distracted
By so many thoughts
The wrong road the falling snow the bell

◆

I wonder if the *Pearl* poet
Was grieving for his lost daughter
Or mourning on commission

For someone else's gem
Whom he turned into a dream vision
Of spotless radiance

I understand the trope the fantasy
Of the erstwhile father the jeweler
Who is so caught

In the chill grip of grief
Over his poor imprisoned pearl
That he falls asleep at her grave

And discovers his precious
As a grown woman
Glittering on the other side

I'm a little rocky on the theology
But I like the idea that a pearl
Is also a two-year-old child

Who is also a royal young woman
Who is also the immortal soul
Who is also the heavenly city

Love could still hurt him
When he awoke in a green garden
Where she lay buried

I wish I could believe in the otherworld
I wish I could believe in a place
Of reunions outside of memory

The *Pearl* poet was baffled
By what he saw in a mound of earth
In the darkened dungeon of sorrow

◆

I do not understand how she could write
Anything but elegies for the stillborn
And God-struck

Margaretha Susanna von Kuntsch
Lost eight sons and five daughters
I do not understand how she could stand

Anything Christian or otherwise
Desperation spoke to me in her voice
And I carried around her poem

Occasioned by the Death of My Fifth Born
Little Son the Little Chrysander or CK
On the 22nd of November 1686

Where she compares herself
To the warrior-king Agamemnon
Since all her hopes and joys

Had burned in the tomb
With her ninth child
Sacrificed to the knife of death

Who will give me the courage
Who will sharpen my crafty pen
When my blood is stirred

To try to describe my feelings in words
I who am merely a woman
My senses falter

My hand trembles
The pen refuses my service
The page is shaking

And cannot bear the words of grief
Let my silent suffering
Bear witness to my desolation

✦

And then all at once
He was sitting across from us
In a booth by the window

In a crowded restaurant
On Route 9 I think
Maybe on Seventy-seventh and Broadway

It was natural to see him
Staring at the menu
And figuring out what to order

Oblivious to the jukebox
And the din around us
His native habitat

Excitement overwhelmed me
And I stared at him so intensely
I almost lit up his face

Don't spook him Laurie said
He doesn't know
What's going to happen

We knew we had seen it all
But he was careless
And didn't understand

You're my only son
I ventured but I couldn't tell
If he heard me over the music

It was so familiar to see him
Sitting across from me again
In the early morning light

It was as simple as daylight
Dawning between us
I could still speak to him

◆

Grief broke down in phrases
And extrapolated lines
From me without myself

Tear-stained pillow of stone
I felt I was lying
Beside him in the coffin

Wormy mother
Who takes us into the ground
With her whenever and wherever

She wants the grass glistens
And grows over us in the heat
Of late summer in the country

It was hard to breathe
When dust choked the treetops
And clotted the roots

Stay calm the light wind blows
Through the branches at night
Peer up at the moon

Not knowing who I am
I was lying beside him
In the coffin I still couldn't breathe

And so I woke up in the shadow
Of morning black light
And put on my mourning clothes

His mother also slipped into black
Treachery of the parents
Who outlive their son

It was too late to warn him
What had already happened
He was going ahead alone

◆

I did not know the work of mourning
Is like carrying a bag of cement
Up a mountain at night

The mountaintop is not in sight
Because there is no mountaintop
Poor Sisyphus grief

I did not know I would struggle
Through a ragged underbrush
Without an upward path

Because there is no path
There is only a blunt rock
With a river to fall into

And Time with its medieval chambers
Time with its jagged edges
And blunt instruments

I did not know the work of mourning
Is a labor in the dark
We carry inside ourselves

Though sometimes when I sleep
I am with him again
And then I wake

Poor Sisyphus grief
I am not ready for your heaviness
Cemented to my body

Look closely and you will see
Almost everyone carrying bags
Of cement on their shoulders

That's why it takes courage
To get out of bed in the morning
And climb into the day

✦

Arriving for the funeral
Disoriented hysterical
It was too much to go through

My mother Gabriel's biggest advocate
Argued that he was a born
Salesman and consumer like her

He had a bit of the con
So what that's necessary in business
She thought I should stake him to a company

You're too tough on him she said
Until she was around him for a few days
And then she thought I wasn't tough enough

I discovered the secret of the bond
Between grandmother and grandson
A common enemy

My sister Nancy and her partner Chelo
His cousin David followed him around
They found him a sweet soul

My sister Lenie too a therapist
He liked to tease her about psychotherapy
Which was *way overrated*

Janet's relatives my cousins and friends
My family wanted to bury him in Chicago
Where he could be near my dad

He wouldn't be so lonesome
Because everyone treks out to visit
On Father's Day and other holidays

But he was a true New Yorker
The city he loved and so we purchased
A plot in Mount Eden Cemetery

✦

Who had always clanged
Like a bell in the darkness
Was now silenced

And I stood in the funeral home
Mute and disbelieving
To bury my son

With the other ritual mourners
My mother my ex-wife my two sisters
My lover in stunned grief

I climbed up a stepladder
To gaze down into his face
Which I touched with my hand

I leaned over and kissed him
On the forehead
It was chilly and hard

I kissed him on the lips
They were stone cold
It was like kissing a corpse

I started keening and wailing
A sob came out of my body
A sound I had never heard before

It was animalistic primal
The wailing the terrible keen
Kept bursting out of me

I wandered off to the side
My relatives cried back and forth
Between the coffin and the pew

Low muffled shrieks and sobs
All the women ringing
Beside themselves

◆

I hope there is a God
Shahid said after his mother died
He owes me an apology

Melville does believe in God
Lawrence Thompson told his class
He thinks He's a real son of a bitch

I solemnly swear before God
That a real Son of a Bitch
Who does not exist

Owes me an apology
Which I will not accept
Anyway I thought the Lord

Cannot help me now or ever
It's a ceremony to say goodbye
The rabbi explained

I do not believe I think
I understand why the old Jews
Tear their clothes and cover the mirrors

Maybe it's not the best time
To think about God's absence
The insensibility of nature

Prayers can help you
Prayers cannot help you
Excessive mourning is forbidden

What else are there but rituals
To cover up the emptiness
O Disbelief

Lord Nothingness
When my son's suffering ended
My own began

◆

Why did the sun rise this morning
It's not natural
I don't want to see the light

It's not time to close the casket
Or say Kaddish for my son
I've already buried two fathers

With a mother to come
Isn't that enough Lord who wants us
To exalt and sanctify Him

I don't want to wear the mourner's ribbon
Or wake up crying every morning
For God knows how long

I don't want to tuck my son into the ground
As if we were putting him to bed
For the last time

Close the prayer book I will not pretend
That God brings peace upon us
And upon all Israel

I don't want to hear anyone
Scolding me from her wheelchair
Because I'm crying too hard

I'm not worried about a heart attack
Nothingness
You've already broken my heart

I will not forgive you
Sun of emptiness
Sky of blank clouds

I will not forgive you
Indifferent God
Until you give me back my son

✦

I was shaking but I was also looking down
At myself from a great distance
Poor grief-stricken father

I pity you I thought
Your heart is lying there
Stretched out in a box

In a Jewish funeral home
And now you must say goodbye
Lamentations forever bereft

The limousines were already lined up
On West End Avenue
For the procession to the cemetery

He would have liked the black sedans
The friends and relatives gathering
Outside the parlor for the funeral

It was time to close the casket
The funeral director said cautiously
There was no more time blanked out

I had to stand on a stepladder
To reach him I couldn't tear myself away
From leaning down and kissing him

On the eyes the forehead the cheeks
The lips colder than ice
The wretched sound

Started coming out of me again
He was there in the coffin
He was not there in the coffin

It was Gabriel it was not Gabriel
Wild spirit beloved son
Where have you fled

✦

ACKNOWLEDGMENTS

My gratitude to Janet Landay, who lived with me through so much of what is recounted here, and has her own story to tell as Gabriel's mother. We have different perspectives, as all parents do, but also a shared history, a united grief.

Thanks to Charles Baxter, Michael Collier, and Garrett Hongo, who have been such rock-solid friends in literature and life. I have great trust in my friend and editor, Deborah Garrison. And I am lucky in my two supportive sisters, Arlene and Nancy Hirsch.

Special thanks to Joseph Straw, whose adventures with Gabriel lift the spirit of this book. Two of the sections adapt his eloquent off-the-cuff eulogy.

Laurie Watel held me up when I needed it most, and inspired me back to life.

This is a father's book, but it belongs to my son Gabriel, who animates it. Some debts are too deep for words.

A NOTE ABOUT THE AUTHOR

Edward Hirsch has published eight books of poetry and five books of prose. He lives in Brooklyn, New York.

A NOTE ON THE TYPE

The text of this book was composed in Palatino, a typeface designed by the noted German typographer Hermann Zapf. Like all Zapf-designed typefaces, Palatino is beautifully balanced and exceedingly readable.

Composed by North Market Street Graphics, Lancaster, Pennsylvania
Printed and bound by Thomson Shore, Dexter, Michigan
Designed by Iris Weinstein

Printed in the United States
by Baker & Taylor Publisher Services